A TRIBUTE TO MOM, WE SURVIVED TOGETHER

BY SAMUEL RIND

AS TOLD TO JANET GOLDMAN

A TRIBUTE TO MOM, WE SURVIVED TOGETHER

iUniverse books may be ordered through booksellers or by contacting:

iUniverse
1663 Liberty Drive
Bloomington, IN 47403
www.iuniverse.com
1-800-Authors (1-800-288-4677)

Because of the dynamic nature of the Internet, any web addresses or links contained in this book may have changed since publication and may no longer be valid. The views expressed in this work are solely those of the author and do not necessarily reflect the views of the publisher, and the publisher hereby disclaims any responsibility for them.

ISBN: 978-1-5320-3003-1 (sc)
ISBN: 978-1-5320-3002-4 (e)

Print information available on the last page.

iUniverse rev. date: 10/02/2017

A TRIBUTE TO MOM, WE SURVIVED TOGETHER

BY SAMUEL RIND
AS TOLD TO JANET GOLDMAN

I dedicate this book to my family, and to the memory of those who have passed away: Mom, Dad, my brother *Naftuli* (Nathan), my aunts, uncles, cousins and grandparents. Additionally, I'm dedicating this book to my wife Gabriela, my son Joseph and his family (my grandkids Nathan and Zanah) and my daughter Brenda.

TABLE OF CONTENTS

PREFACE

I'm no hero. Yet, I'd like to share my lifetime experiences. Through this book and presentations, I hope to affect as many people as possible. Being a Holocaust survivor, I've witnessed outlandishly inhuman behavior. By helping others to understand the past as well as the importance of education, awareness, appreciation and support of human rights, I hope we can all say, "Never again!"

It's difficult for me to write about the past. Some people don't realize how hard it is for me to tell my story. I usually joke around. That's the way I am. It's the way I relax. Painful memories are always there. When the war broke out, September 1, 1939, I was only two years old. Consequently, I needed to depend upon my mom's recollections for many of the details provided in this memoir. Some of the events were so traumatic that even as a child, they engraved themselves on my consciousness. People have asked "Why don't you have a tattoo on your arm?" Only the Jews who were in the Auschwitz Concentration Camp were numbered; some were not. The numbers were part of an inventory system to keep track of how many were killed.

It is important for me to acknowledge that the writing of my memoir, as well as Mom's, would have been extremely difficulty without the help of others. Barbara Appelbaum, as director of the Rochester Jewish Federation's Center for Holocaust Awareness and Information (CHAI), since retired, interviewed me about 19 years ago and made a tape to be kept for future generations at the USC Shoah Foundation. Additionally, Barbara assisted me with verbally presenting my story to community groups and encouraged me to write my own memoir. Bonnie Abrams, the new CHAI director, continued to assist me with arranging presentations.

Through networking, Bonnie introduced Janet Goldman to Barbara for assisting with the Rochester Holocaust Survivors' Website. Knowing of my interest in publishing a book, Barbara connected Janet to me for assisting with this project. Barbara shared my interview summaries, the typed and taped versions, a collection of my photos, Mom's memoir and a few historical articles. Additionally, Barbara suggested topics for further development. In particular, she suggested expanding upon my transformation which allowed me to lead a normal and happy life. Clearly, Janet and I valued and appreciated Barbara's contributions.

When writing this memoir, I occasionally used Yiddish words. When doing so, I used italics and added the English translation in parentheses for each word's initial usage.

ACKNOWLEDGEMENTS

I'd like to acknowledge the assistance of many people. First of all, I'd like to thank my wife, Gabriela, for her encouragement. I'd also like to thank my son, Joseph and daughter, Brenda, for their support. Of course, I'd like to thank Mom who helped with my memories. Using her memoir, I was better able to retell our experiences of my early years. I would also like to thank Debbie Rothman for translating my mother's memoir.

I'd like to thank Janet Goldman for her assistance with writing this memoir. She has done an outstanding job. For the graphic design, I must thank Shauna Goldman. She transformed my memoir into a reader friendly format, simplifying the maps, and expertly formatting the photos, and text. I'd also like to thank Lior Burg, Meghan Hanson-Peters, Sarah Krieger and Tom Zigon for some of the photographs.

I'd like to thank Barbara Appelbaum for not giving up on me and making sure I told my story.

I'd like to thank Richard Gordon and Keith Greer for providing background information about the "Journey for Identity" program. For sharing their perspectives of the trip experience, I'd like to thank: Lior Burg, Rachel Cardiel, Sarah Krieger, Ben Richardson, Daniel Silver, and Seth Silver.

I'd like to thank Stacy Cougle, Tara DeVay, Meghan Hanson-Peters, Dr. Robert Ike, Joe Tobia and Marcia Weber for providing background information about my presentations.

For testimonials about the book, I'd like to thank: Bonnie Abrams, Stacy Cougle, Tara DeVay, Meghan Hanson-Peters and Rabbi Leonardo Bitran.

For editing assistance, I'd like to thank: Bonnie Abrams, Stacy Cougle, Meghan Hanson-Peters and Tara DeVay.

I'd also like to thank the publishing team at iUniverse.

Publication of this book was made possible through a generous grant of the Anna Suss Paull Family Fund of the Foundation of the Jewish Federation of Greater Rochester. I would also like to thank Bonnie Abrams, the Jewish Federation's Director of the Center for Holocaust Awareness and Information for her invaluable assistance.

FAMILY TREE – MOM'S FAMILY

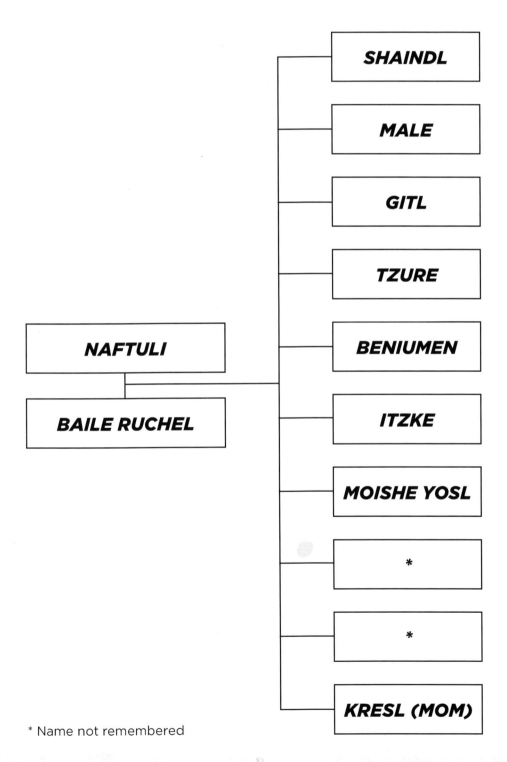

NAFTULI

BAILE RUCHEL

SHAINDL

MALE

GITL

TZURE

BENIUMEN

ITZKE

MOISHE YOSL

*

*

KRESL (MOM)

* Name not remembered

FAMILY TREE - DAD'S FAMILY

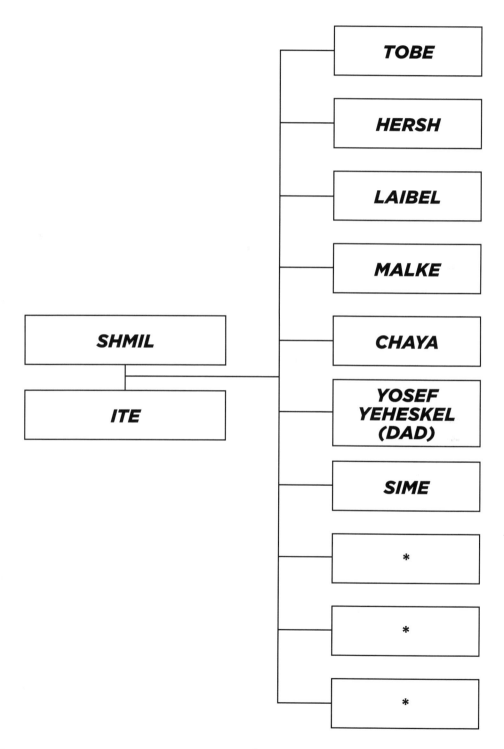

1940
MAY 17
My brother,
Naftuli, was born.

1941
JULY
We fled to
Rava-Ruska and
then to Breslau,
Germany.

1937
I was born in
Krasnobród-Lubelski,
Poland.

1944
MARCH
We were liberated by
soldiers from Uzbekistan
and Kazakstan. We went
back to Poland, to a
town called Bielawa and
joined a kibbutz.

1935

1945

1

1939
SEPTEMBER
German troops invaded
Krasnobród-Lubelski;
my family fled to
Tomaszow-Lubelski,
Poland.

1942
We were taken to
Rachney and then
to Pechora, back
and forth, in the
Ukraine. Dad and
Naftuli were killed.

1945
SUMMER
We traveled to
Czechoslovakia and
then onto Staiern,
Austria where we
lived in an American
displaced persons
camp.

1943
FEBRUARY/MARCH
We escaped to Zhmerinka.

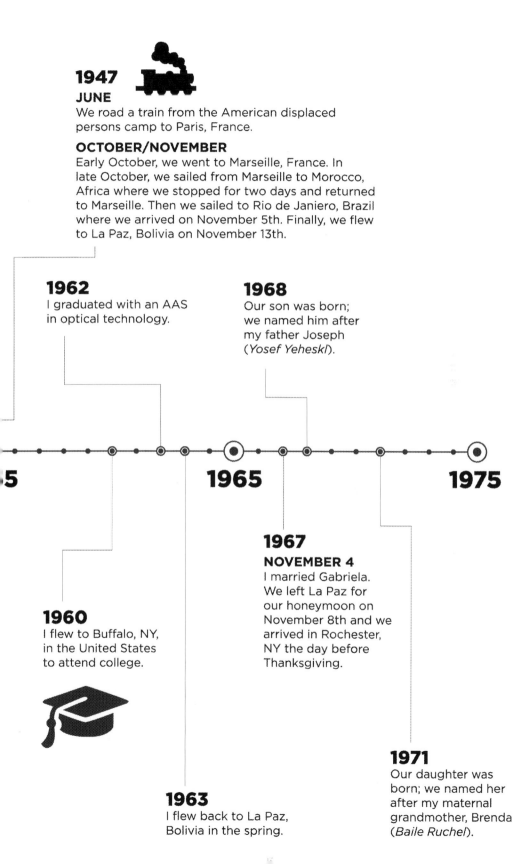

1947
JUNE
We road a train from the American displaced persons camp to Paris, France.

OCTOBER/NOVEMBER
Early October, we went to Marseille, France. In late October, we sailed from Marseille to Morocco, Africa where we stopped for two days and returned to Marseille. Then we sailed to Rio de Janiero, Brazil where we arrived on November 5th. Finally, we flew to La Paz, Bolivia on November 13th.

1962
I graduated with an AAS in optical technology.

1968
Our son was born; we named him after my father Joseph (*Yosef Yeheskl*).

5

1965

1975

1967
NOVEMBER 4
I married Gabriela. We left La Paz for our honeymoon on November 8th and we arrived in Rochester, NY the day before Thanksgiving.

1960
I flew to Buffalo, NY, in the United States to attend college.

1971
Our daughter was born; we named her after my maternal grandmother, Brenda (*Baile Ruchel*).

1963
I flew back to La Paz, Bolivia in the spring.

1 FAMILY BACKGROUND

I was born on June 12, 1937 in Krasnobród-Lubelski, a small Polish town near Lublin, 180 miles southeast of Warsaw. At birth, my name was *Shmuel* Rind and was later "Mila;" that's what they used to call me in Russia. My parents were *Yosef Yeheskel* Rind and *Kresl* Walter Rind. Dad was born in December of 1903. Mom was born March 13, 1912. I had one brother, *Naftuli*, who was born in 1940. Although my immediate family was small, my extended family was large, very close knit and religious, almost Hasidic (ultra religious).

Dad was born in Krasnobród-Lubelski. He had nine siblings. Two brothers went to Israel during or after the war. One of the two eventually continued onto America, more specifically, he ended up in New Jersey. One sister survived the Holocaust and ended up in Munich, Germany with her husband and son. The other six siblings perished during the Holocaust.

Dad, before he married Mom

Mom was born in the *shtetl* (small Jewish town) of Józefów-Bilgorajski, where she lived until 1936 when she married my dad. Józefów-Bilgorajski was 10 or less miles away from Krasnobród-Lubelski. Mom had nine siblings. Except for one sister, born after my mother turned five, they were all older. Before Mom was born, her father sent four of her siblings, one brother and three sisters, to America, Brooklyn, New York because they didn't act according to his religious beliefs. Such behavior was seriously offensive to Mom's father as he was a very religious man, a *Melamed* (teacher of teachers). Rabbis came to him for discussions and advice. Yet, it was *bashert* (God's will) that this banishment to America became the opposite, an opportunity to escape the Holocaust.

One of Mom's brothers was drafted into the Polish army, around 1929 or 1930. He escaped from the barracks and found his way to Montreal, Canada. Another brother, one of the four siblings who had been sent to America, rented a car and picked him up in Montreal and drove him back to New York.

Still another one of Mom's brothers, *Moishe Yosl* (Moses), escaped to Bolivia. During February 1939, the army started drafting every healthy man up to 45 years of age, in alphabetical order. That is when my grandmother dressed him up as a woman and sent him to safety in March of 1939. She took him to Warsaw where he took a train to Paris, France. From France, he took a ship to Chile and then a train to La Paz, Bolivia. Before leaving, he promised his wife and daughter that he'd come back for them. However, some time after the war started, the neighbors reported his wife and daughter; they were subsequently murdered. Mom's three other siblings were killed in Europe in 1941-1942.

Traveling documents for my Uncle Moishe Yosl

Mom, before the war

Mom was a remarkable woman. When she was a child, women were not entitled to learn about religion. By hiding behind the curtains, and listening to her father, she knew the prayer book, inside out and the meaning, by the age of eight. Similarly, she knew the Chumash, the Five Books of Moses (or the Torah). She taught me more about religion than my religious school teachers. Mom dropped out of school in seventh grade because she needed to help her mother with the family business, a liquor business; her father died of a brain hemorrhage. Their best customer was the Chief of Police.

Although Mom's education was limited, she was very bright with tremendous common sense. Frequently, through her management of our daily challenges during the Holocaust, she demonstrated her cleverness and stamina. Mom developed ideas without even thinking. She would just go ahead and do it. That's why I fell in love with the Nike commercial, "Just do it!" Sometimes with the human brain, too much thinking makes things worse. Mom didn't say much, but what she said was clever. Mom didn't yell. It was all in her eyes. How do you explain a Jewish mother?! I'm thinking of the song, *"The Yiddishe Momme"* (The Jewish Mother). Sometimes, she used killer eyes to relay her message.

When reliving her experiences during the Holocaust, Mom would become agitated. Nevertheless, one day, she gathered her courage and began to write her memories in her native Yiddish. Off and on, between the 1950s and 1980s, she wrote her memoir. First, she wrote about how troubling this task was. In fact, she hoped to consult with some special Israeli Holocaust committee. This group included survivors from four to five towns; Mom could have been a member. She thought this committee could help her fill in the gaps. However, we never contacted that committee, we only talked about it.

Uncle Moishe Yosl

Letter From Aunt Rachel, (In Poland), To Her Husband, Uncle *Moishe Yosl* (In Bolivia), May 28, 1940, (Handwritten In Polish)

Beloved Husband,

I received your letter on May 26, 1940. When I received your letter, my heart as well the hearts of parents, family and the entire city were filled with happiness knowing that you are healthy. Goldsztajnowa (postal clerk) received a number of letters already but I have not received any letters from you until now. I was embarrassed to go and ask her (postal clerk) if there is anything for me. People from the entire city were making fun of me. They said that you left me and you don't even want to write to me. We all are healthy thank God, but your parents are not in Jozefowie.

Our daughter is as pretty as a little doll, big blue eyes, and light hair, very beautiful face. Balcia can say "daddy." When I read your letter, she grabs it from my hands all the time as if she would know that the letter is from her father. When I will have more patience, I will take her picture and I will send it to you.

Please tell me what do you sell and how is life treating you? Please send me your picture from the last few months because I would like to see how you look now.

I don't have anything else to write. Please write back soon. I wrote two letters to you before I got yours. I am sending you greetings from parents, brother, Cousin Azryla and all our friends.

I am greeting you from far away, your loving wife,
Rachela Walter
Jozefow, May 28, 1940

SAM'S TRAVELS THROUGH EUROPE, 1937-1947

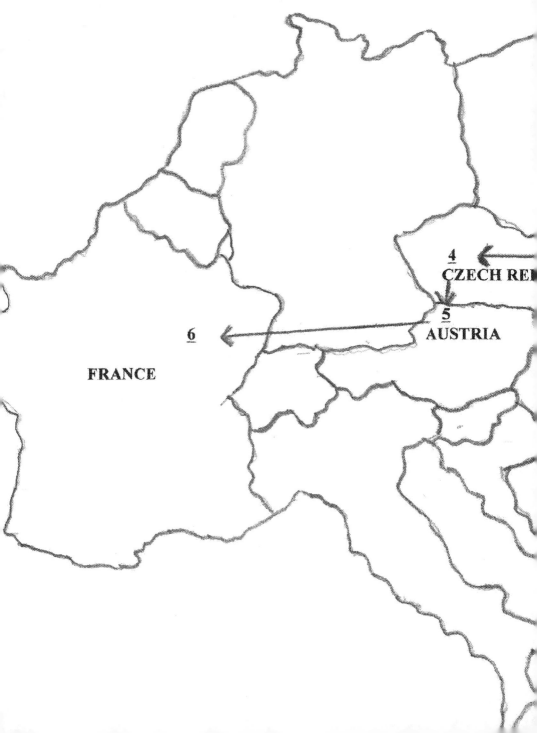

OLAND 1

3

2

UKRAINE

2 LIFE IN KRASNOBRÓD-LUBELSKI

In Krasnobród-Lubelski, we lived on the same street as our synagogue and many of our relatives. The synagogue was next to my Dad's uncle's house and my grandmother lived on the other side of the synagogue. We shared the home of Dad's sister. Dad and my aunt owned and worked in a bakery. This bakery used to belong to their parents. They also owned a farm with horses and some cows. The farm was located on the outskirts of Krasnobród-Lubelski. I liked riding the horses. It came easily to me even though I was so young. In fact, Mom used to say that I "was born on a horse." To this day, I like watching equestrians. I also have memories of playing with Dad, while sitting on his lap. Mom, I can remember, was often busy cleaning.

December 1938

Mom referred to Krasnobród-Lubelski as a *shtetl* (a small town). Back in 1921, with a population of 2,036, 1,148, were Jewish.[1] The first Jews lived there in the second half of the 16th century.[2] At that time, most worked in trades and crafts.[3] In the 19th and 20th centuries, Jews still worked in the trades and crafts, but also leased forests and orchards and some sold timber, grain or cattle.[4]

As elsewhere in Poland and Europe, Krasnobród-Lubelski's anti-Semitism worsened in the 1930's. The town's Jews experienced an economic boycott and anti-Jewish riots.[5] I believe the townspeople were acting out of jealousy and envy. Jewish families tended to have secure livelihoods; they were savers, hard workers and family focused. In the fall of 1937, there was also a blood libel case where Jews were blamed for the death of a 10 year-old Christian girl.[6]

On September 13, 1939, the eve of the Jewish New Year, the German army entered the town. Soldiers began fighting in the streets. At the time, I was two-years-old. Bullets were flying between the Polish and German armies. Mom remembered looking out the window and seeing bullets kill civilians in the middle of the town square. The authorities posted signs requiring men to report for military duty. Mom was afraid that Dad would be drafted into the army. Within ten days, the Germans occupied our town. They searched for food. Since Dad and my aunt owned the bakery, the Germans searched our home first, taking food without leaving us anything. When other Jews came to our door asking for food, we had nothing left to offer. In her memoir, Mom wrote "How depressing it was. We did not even have a crumb of bread."

Our homes became crowded with Jewish refugees. By foot and horse-drawn wagons, refugees came from different towns. In her memoir, Mom described them: "They came from Galicia, fleeing from the Germans. They described terrible things that one could not believe at first, that is until we finally began to comprehend." Consequently, people began to flee from their homes. From our house, the Krakow refugees fled first. My parents, with my uncles and aunts discussed how we should try to stick together as we leave Krasnobród-Lubelski. On the other hand, they also discussed the need to separate; if we all stayed together and were caught, we'd all be dead. Dad's youngest brother, who was probably in his early 20s at the time, suggested what became the agreed upon solution: we should divide into groups of ten. Our group included Mom, Dad, Mom's sister and her husband, their four daughters, me, and eventually, *Naftuli*. My two sets of grandparents had already passed away by then. We left, bringing only a few possessions in something comparable to pillowcases. I can't remember what my mother packed, maybe some clothes, utensils, and a photo of me when I was 18 months old.

In September 1939, we fled through nearby fields and woods to the house of a Polish acquaintance. With several families, we stayed for a short while until the shooting came too close. Together with non-Jews, we ran into the forest. To hide from the bombing, we used trenches left from the partisans and made trenches of our own. While we were choosing to hide in the trenches, others fled back to their homes. No one knew where it would be safe.

When we heard that the Germans were pushed back, we returned home with many others thinking that it was safer. But no one slept that night. We had officers in our home as well as the homes of my aunts and uncles. Our *shtetl* was occupied by Polish soldiers. At dawn, shooting resumed. We ran from our home and into the forest, back into the trenches. As described by Mom, "A day or two go by, until a few Jews from our town, Krasnobród-Lubelski, appear and they tell horrible things about what the Germans are doing to our people. They take them to work, and it is impossible to describe the torture. So we remain where we are. The shooting begins to quiet down. The gentiles return to the houses, but we Jews lie together, several families, and wonder what we should do. Go back to town into the hands of the Germans?"

Soon after, two Polish soldiers arrived, claiming to be Jewish and asked us for civilian clothing. These soldiers told us they would hide with us for a few days before returning to the town. In two days, they expected Russians would be arriving. These soldiers were right, Russians did come to our *shtetl*. However, as explained by Mom, before the Germans left, "they doused the Jewish homes with gasoline, and set them on fire. All that was left were a few houses on Tomaszów Street. And these were quickly crammed with the few people who returned to town." One hundred and ninety-eight Jews lost their lives during the days since the Germans entered Krasnobród-Lubelski.[7]

When we came back to our town, we no longer had a home; others were living in it. Instead we searched for another house where we could rent a room. The non-Jews refused us saying "If the Germans return, we cannot have Jews in our house." There were a few homes with Jews; they were so crowded that we lay head to head. Knowing that we would have to flee, without our belongings, Dad hid some of our valuables on the outskirts of Krasnobród-Lubelski. The hiding spots must have been quite a distance from the town. Dad always took a long time to get there. However, I never knew if some of the travel time was due to Dad hiding from danger.

1 Morris Gradel, "Pinkas Hakehillot Polin: Krasnobrod," *Encyclopaedia of Jewish Communities in Poland,*vol. 7, Aug. 2003, Yad Vashem, accessed 2 Aug. 2016, www.jewishgen.org/yizkor/pinkas_pland/pol7_00513.html, 513-515.
2 Ibid.
3 Ibid.
4 Ibid.
5 Ibid.
6 Ibid.
7 Ibid.

3
FLEEING TO
TOMASZÓW-LUBELSKI

We were only able to stay in Krasnobród-Lubelski a few days before we had to leave again. Three weeks had passed since the war began in our hometown. The Russians planned to evacuate as they knew the Germans were returning. Not wanting to abandon us, the Russians offered to drive people as far as Rava-Ruska. Dad's brother, *Leybush*, and his family left, but Dad refused as he didn't want to leave without the rest of our family. On Hoshana Raba, the 7th day of Sukkot (a Jewish harvest holiday) in October, Dad arranged for us to leave with one aunt, uncle and their four daughters.

We walked through fields and woods to Tomaszów-Lubelski where my grandfather's brother and my grandmother's sister lived. The towns were close to each other, probably about ten miles apart. Although the distance was not bad, the weather added another challenge; we were having a heavy rainstorm. Soaked, we arrived at my great aunt's home. She was still there with one son. We were so happy to be together. When we first arrived, Tomaszów-Lubelsi was not yet a ghetto. We all lived together in that house where I think my brother was born on May 17, 1940. According to certain documentation, he might have been born in Breslau (Wroclaw) where we later traveled. Because of the war, and lack of records, we're not sure.

In 1931, Tomaszów-Lubelski had 10,403 inhabitants with 5,669 Jews.[1] However, as in other parts of Europe, the 1930s brought anti-Semitism and violence. There were pogroms, violence where people demolish, destroy and kill. These pogroms were aimed at Jews. Before we arrived, on September 6, 1939, the Germans bombarded the town, badly affecting the Jewish section.[2] On September 13th, the Germans came into the town and forced Jews, aged 12 to 50, into slave labor, heavy construction including digging.[3] On September 20th, the Germans left and were replaced by Russians. A week later, when the Soviet troops left, many Jews joined them, leaving 3,500 Jews.[4] Germans returned and again forced Jews into slave labor. I remember my mother working. She used to carry heavy supplies. However, due to her pregnancy, she eventually had to stop working.

By December 1939, all Jews, 12 years of age and older had to wear yellow armbands with the Star of David. I remember having to wear these yellow patches on my outer garments. Often Jews had to make their own patches. I don't remember if Mom made mine. Within a year, Tomaszów-Lubelski eventually became a ghetto. The Jews were required to move to two streets in the town. Our home had to hold four families. It was an open ghetto; people could leave to work or to barter for food and other needs. People managed, they were able to get enough necessities to survive. The synagogue was within the ghetto walls; it was an actual synagogue, not just a room in a building.

Traveling from Krasnobród-Lubelski to Tomaszów-Lubelski

In July 1941, the Germans crossed the border into Poland; bombing and shooting began, again. People were fleeing from one town to another. Some fled on foot, others by small carts. Mom, her sister and her sister's daughters thought we should leave. However, Dad and my Uncle *Leybush* disagreed; they thought we should stay. They further discussed this dilemma with Abraham Gortler and *Berkeh* Vinder, men from the community who were elders and friends. Dad changed his mind at the synagogue where he met Jews from other towns. Mom wrote, "My husband comes home with the cousin and they are unable to speak. After they calm down a bit, they say that there were Jews in the synagogue from towns already occupied by the Germans and that it is impossible to describe the horrible things they do to our people. It is decided to move on again." We also learned that non-Jews were volunteering by the millions to help the Nazis as they took over the European countries. Without formal organization, non-Jews went up to the authorities and volunteered their services. They helped round up Jews or others, taking them into the woods and shooting them. People turned in their own neighbors.

Morris "Gradel, "Pinkas Hakehillot Polin: Tomaszow Lubelski," Encyclopedia of Jewish Communities in Poland, vol. 7, Aug. 2003, Yad Vashem, accessed 2 Aug. 2016, www. jewishgen.org/Yiskor/pinkas_poland/pol7_00237b.html, 237-241.
2 Ibid.
3 Ibid.
4 Ibid.

4 ONWARD TO RAVA-RUSKA

We left Tomaszów-Lubelski and again wandered and took trains until we reached Rava-Ruska in the Ukraine, near the Polish border. I was four; *Naftuli* was two. Before we reached Rava-Ruska, Germans had occupied the town for a few weeks. The Germans formed a *Judenrat* (Jewish council in occupied territory) in July to keep a census, supply them with forced labor crews, and valuables. This Judenrat was also able to help the Jews with material supplies such as soup kitchens and medical aid. However, the primary purpose was to help the Germans. Their lives depended upon their allegiance.

When we arrived in Rava-Ruska, we found the town's Jews would not let us in; their homes, synagogues and houses of study were already crowded with men, women and children. Mom wrote in her memoir, "The Rava Ruska Jews would not let anyone in and kept their doors shut. Their answer to our knocking was, 'You should not have left your homes.' Outside, it was as cold and rainy as it was in our hearts." Finally, Mom found someone who let *Naftuli* into bed with her daughter and gave us something to eat; this was after she heard that Mom was from Józefów-Bilgorajski. At night, we returned to Dad. That night, we slept on the ground or on the floor somewhere. Dad managed to get us food. The next day, Mom searched for a cousin from Tomaszów-Lubelski whose stepdaughter held an important position under Soviet rule. Mom spoke to this daughter, who arranged a housing permit. We shared this house with a few other families who had arrived before us. The house had belonged to a Jewish family who fled earlier. Mom described the house, "We opened our eyes and felt as if we had entered the Garden of Eden. What a miracle to have a roof over one's head." We were so happy to have a roof, warmth and even some food. We were able to get a potato, a beet and a carrot.

Within a few days, *Moyshe* Printz, a friendly community leader, came to our door and brought us to the high school where, by luck, we located our family from Krasnobród-Lubelski; they had arrived only two days earlier. We found Mom's sister Sarah with her four children. Since Aunt Sarah's husband was in Belarus, we arranged for them to travel deep into Russia to be with each other. Our bed was the floor, where we slept covered by something, I don't remember what. While staying in that high school, my little brother, *Naftuli*, became very sick. *Moyshe* Printz ran with one of my aunts to get a doctor. This doctor helped my brother to recover.

Soon after our arrival, we were told to leave; there wasn't room for out-of-town people like us. Dad and my uncle went to the town's Russian commander for assistance. However, this commander told them that all of the refugees had to leave. Our choice was to voluntarily take a train to the Ukraine or else be sent to Siberia. Naturally, Dad and my uncle chose the Ukraine. We all left for the train station. Upon arriving at the station, *Avrom* Gorler, a member of the community, called Dad to get in the boxcar with his family and *Berkeh* Vinder, another community member. We travelled in these freight cars for three days, with no food.

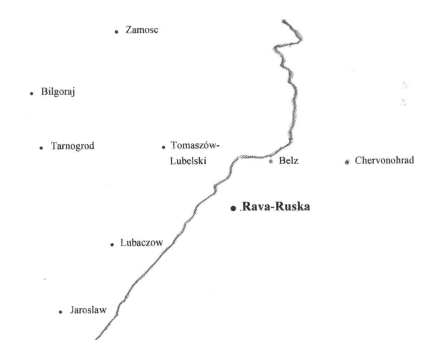

Traveling from Tomaszów-Lubelski to the Region of Rava-Ruska

5

MOVING
TO BRESLAU

The train took us to Breslau by the German border. Soon after we arrived, Jewish officials took us to a house with furniture. They even brought us food and drink. We were very grateful. In her memoir, Mom wrote "We open our eyes and thank God for the grace that we saved our lives; we begin to live like other people in Russia." By standing in queues, we were able to get more food and other things as needed. Mom found the address of her sister, Sarah and her family. By sending them documents, Sarah, her husband *Leybish* Bristman and their children were able to come live with us in February of 1942.

The Germans repeatedly came to our house and demanded different things, mainly food. Mom wrote "whatever we had, we gave them just so that they would spare our lives." From a window, Mom watched as the Germans burned Torah scrolls. After a short while, the Germans chose a section of the town as a Jewish ghetto. Christians had to leave and Jews had to squeeze in. Jews were not allowed outside of the ghetto, under penalty of death. The Germans surrounded the ghetto with barbed wire. We had already been living in the designated area. Since we had a few rooms, the Germans squeezed in two more families, totaling four families.

We created a hiding place in this house for all of us. After throwing a little bedding and food into a dark room, we shut and hid the door. The room's entrance became the area underneath a cupboard in the floor, a place that wouldn't be noticed. Being only two years old, my brother didn't like the darkness of the hiding place, he cried constantly while in that room. So the others ordered Mom and my brother to leave. Consequently, my parents, brother and I left the hiding place. The authorities sent us to Rachney, by truck. At that time, I was about five years old; it was early in 1942.

# 6

SENT TO RACHNEY

Rachney was a small labor camp in the Ukraine and most of the guards weren't German but Ukranian or Romanian. The workers had to build storage sheds, or chop stones. These stones were to be used for covering graves. When Mom worked, she left me with other children who were under 12 or 13; the older ones had to dig graves for the dead from Rachney and other camps. In these graves, they buried people, one on top of the other. Children, ages 6 to 11, moved and chopped stones. The younger ones like me were kept busy by doing activities like picking up and moving stones. The older children supervised the younger children.

In Rachney, like earlier towns, we experienced the Judenrat. My parents learned to be careful of them. Judenrat members were fed well and given decent clothes. In return, they turned people in to be exterminated or reported people who were plotting things. I remember on one occasion when Mom attempted to take me somewhere and a Judenrat leader began to hit her. In Rachney, I also remember seeing someone get hit with a shovel by a guard, probably for not moving fast enough. Some people who were near-dead were killed on the spot by gun or by heavy tools such as shovels or crowbars. Then there were those who were made to dig their own grave, and were buried alive.

When given food, we were fed leftovers or even horse feed. From whatever camp we were in, Dad would leave at night, to get more food or goods that could be exchanged for food. Sometimes he snuck out with Mom's brother-in-law. Even Mom didn't know how he managed. He returned to that hiding spot outside of Krasnobród-Lubelski where he had buried some of our possessions. Some of those belongings may still be buried. He'd make exchanges with the people on the other side of the fence. For example, he exchanged an 18 karat gold ring for a potato. That one potato was divided so many ways among the four of us. Mom gave the meat of the potato to *Naftuli*. She gave me the skin. And the broth, she shared with Dad. Back then, I could go for days without food.

SENT TO PECHORA

From Rachney, we were trucked to Pechora, also in the Ukraine. Like yo-yos, we were bounced around between different camps in 1942. Each time, we dreaded returning to Pechora. It began as a holding camp where people stayed until the authorities shipped them elsewhere. Over time, Pechora became a death camp where people starved to death or were murdered. We couldn't stay in the work camps when we were sick. One of the times, we became sick from eating horse feed. The Nazi leaders didn't send the residents to work, but didn't provide food either.

Upon our arrival, two of Dad's siblings and their families were taken from the camp and never heard from again. In front of us, the guards shot the two eldest daughters of Mom's sister; her husband was killed separately. Mom's sister's two younger children died from starvation. My parents, my brother and I became the only members of the Rind family at this location. What was left of my extended family had become scattered.

Pechora was considered to be an experimental camp.[1] The Nazis experimented for ways to run similar camps more effectively, minimizing resources to exterminate a greater number of people. Unlike concentration camps with gas chambers, Pechora's administrators arranged death by starvation. The residents were stuffed into close quarters, using all available space including hallways, bathrooms, underground cellars and barracks.[2] With concrete floors, and dirt floors, no heating, lice and fleas, the living conditions were horrible.[3]

Ironically, Pechora was originally built as a "private estate" with lots of trees.[4] It later became a sanitorium before becoming a Romanian administered camp in December of 1941.[5] The camp was located in the village of Pechora, beside the Bug River, in the Tulchin area of Vinnitsa Oblast.[6]

Survivors' memories vary regarding whether the surrounding stone and concrete walls were topped with barbed wire. Similar to my father's nighttime escapes for food, other survivors remember climbing the walls. Some remembered piling stones next to the walls to help, while some resorted to digging ditches under the walls.[7] Another method was to wade through the Bug River next to which the walls were positioned.[8] As Ukrainian police might be positioned on the wall's other side, this was a dangerous process.[9] Some of the other survivor testimonies reported observations of the extreme mental effects of starvation, a few examples of cannibalistic activity.[10] Mom and I never observed such activity, but we had heard rumors. In fact, that's why we quickly buried my brother after his death.

One day, in November, Dad left for another search for items to exchange for food. Several weeks passed since he left. During that time, I had become the "man of the house." Although I was only five years old, I grew up faster and realized that I must protect my mom. I did this by following her around as much as I could. I tried to make sure that she was OK. For example, I would help her lift heavy stones.

Even though Pechora was not an extermination camp, three weeks after we lost Dad, my brother, two years and eight months old, was killed. In front of me, a Ukrainian guard, with a yellow stick, hit *Naftuli* on the head, murdering him. At the time, *Naftuli* was crying in Mom's arms, leaning on her shoulders. The guard warned Mom to stop *Naftuli* from crying; screaming, he said "If you don't stop him, I will." *Naftuli* was already fragile; he was malnourished and dying from starvation. Regardless, the violent act was despicable. His life was snatched up right before my eyes. No one should have to witness a horrendous senseless act of violence such as this. No parent should have to bury their child. Afterwards, Mom had to carry *Naftuli* to the house for the dead where we buried him. I will never forget how the dead bodies looked. Touching a dead body shakes you all over. It felt like a current running through my body.

That was the end of my childhood. Since then, until I was ten years old, whenever I saw or heard the footsteps of a man in uniform, I would hide behind Mom as I feared another guard was coming to murder us. I still have nightmares, 70 plus years later. I try not to let that memory interfere with my life. *Naftuli's* murder left an indelible mark on my soul that will remain with me forever. Also at my young age back then, I learned to read people by their eyes and body movement. To this day, I still rely heavily upon these nonverbal cues to determine a person's credibility and honesty.

By the middle of December (1942), Dad still had not come back from his nighttime search for food or goods. Dad had been gone a month. Mom didn't know if he had died.

1 Rebecca L. Golbert, "Holocaust Sites in Ukraine: Pechora and the Politics of Memorialization," Holocaust & Genocide Studies Journal," vol. 18, issue 2, Oxford University Press, 2004, 215.
2 Ibid., pp. 219-222.
3 Ibid., pp. 219-220.
4 Ibid. p. 206.
5 Ibid., p. 206.
6 Ibid., p. 223.
7 Rebecca L. Golbert, "Holocaust Sites in Ukraine: Pechora and the Politics of Memorialization," Holocaust & Genocide Studies Journal," vol. 18, issue 2, Oxford University Press, 2004, 216.
8 Ibid.
9 Ibid.
10 Ibid., 215.

8 ESCAPE TO ZHMERINKA

In the fall of 1943, Mom and I escaped to a ghetto in the Ukrainian city of Zhmerinka. This was made possible by one of Dad's sisters; she had learned of our whereabouts by talking to the Freedom Fighters in her ghetto. The Freedom Fighters were a network of people, known as the Polish Underground, and/or Jewish Resistance Fighters. One of their many activities was making grenades by filling toys, baby dolls, and such with dynamite. They left these grenades in the woods for Nazis to step on and be blown to hell. Another activity was when they traveled in and out of camps, risking their lives to tell people in camps to not give up hope. While in the camps, they tried recruiting more fighters. Through their travels, they became a source of information.

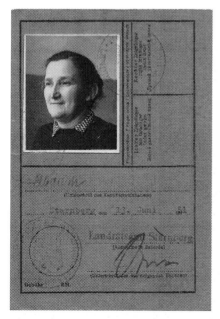

Passport of my Aunt Chaya, Dad's sister; she helped us escape to Zhmerinka where we lived with her, Uncle Benjamin and Cousin Leibl.

Dad's brother-in-law was able to arrange for the assistance of Rachel, a stranger who was a Jewish resistance fighter; she volunteered to help. She was a beautiful young Jewish woman who didn't look Jewish; she looked like a typical farm girl with blonde hair and blue eyes. This young woman knew us from Breslau. At Rachney, another inmate alerted Mom to Rachel's presence by the fence. Through Mom's conversation with Rachel, they arranged for our departure. To prepare, Mom got hold of some linen and made a giant scarf to bundle me up. With the scarf, I wouldn't look like a boy but a good-looking little girl. Having been circumcised, I could easily be identified as a Jew. In Poland, non-Jews were not circumcised. It would have been

Aunt Chaya and her son, Leibl, in front of their apartment complex in Munich, Germany, late 1950's/early 1960's. Leibl needed special services due to the fact that he was playing with a grenade and a nail (he thought it was a dud) while living in Zhmerinka in 1944 before we were liberated. Usually, I sat on his lap, but not that day. He was totally blind and missing his left forearm and hand, and two fingers on his right hand. Leibl spent part of each year in Israel and Germany.

Cousin Leibl, in front of the apartment complex., 1980s

dangerous if guards stopped us and thought I was a boy. The three of us would have been killed.

At nighttime, we met Rachel and walked through the gates which were not well guarded. Due to fear of the unknown, most Jews didn't leave the camp. We didn't bring anything but what we were wearing. As we could only travel at night, it took us at least three days to get to our destination. I remember there was snow on the ground. For one of the nights, we stopped at a house that seemed to be in the middle of nowhere. A scared couple pulled us in. It turned out that they were Romanian Jews and somehow were able to get this little house. We couldn't stay long. For food, we did with what my aunt and uncle gave to Rachel, one and a half loaves of bread (we managed). Had she carried more, she would have appeared to be traveling and would have been stopped and questioned.

Whenever we travelled between towns, we used indirect routes to avoid being noticed. Walking through woods was often like walking through cemeteries. The Nazis took people to the woods and shot them, covering them with stones stolen from cemeteries. Guards stopped us three times. Rachel's beauty saved us; the guards looked at her and not at Mom and me. Thanks to Rachel, we made it to Zhmerinka, safely. Rachel risked her life because of her family history; the Nazis killed her entire family. I later learned that Rachel emigrated to Israel and died fighting in the War of Independence (1948).

Zhmerinka was a city in the Ukraine. In 1926, 5,186 Jews, or one-third of the population, lived in this city.[1] During World War II, it became part of the Romanian occupation zone. Jewish refugees fled to Zhmerinka from surrounding districts as well as Jews who were expelled from Romania. Then there were Jews who fled from Zhmerinka because in many situations, Jews didn't know which way was safe. They ran in all directions. By June of 1942, the number of Jews totaled 3,274 and they were all constrained into the city's ghetto.[2] In March of 1943, Jews were forced to work at and near the railway station, a war supply factory.[3]

In Zhmerinka, our lifestyle improved considerably. Still not knowing where Dad was, we stayed with my Aunt *Chaya* and Uncle Benjamin as well as my cousin, *Leibl*, who was 11 years older than me. Together, we all stayed in the home of one wealthy Jew, Kutzenko, where my aunt and uncle were staying. This wealthy man managed to have special living arrangements for other people as well. While the guards continued to investigate where his wealth was hidden, they protected him from the authorities. Kutzenko had cleverly hidden his gold in the walls of his home. We lived upstairs where I shared a room with Mom. My aunt and Mom did the cooking; Kutzenko bought the food. Although it was a ghetto, the adults could work within their respective professions. My uncle worked as a boot maker. He had been a boot maker since the age of 16 and was very good at his profession. My uncle specialized in luxury boots, for people who had money.

Although Zhmerinka was such an improvement over Pechora, it was still a town where Jews were subjected to forced labor. My uncle was able to avoid forced labor. Prior to the town becoming a ghetto, he had

Map of Zhmerinka; Pechora is 30 miles southeast of Zhmerinka.[4]

established his business; he had good contacts and wealthy clients. To satisfy the appropriate political officials, he occasionally spent time teaching his skills.

Mom worked very hard in a factory which made parts for trucks. Every day, she had to go to work, even when it was very cold, 20°F. Once when she didn't feel well, she went to see the Jewish Romanian doctor; he was the head of the ghetto and the Judenrat. This doctor told Mom that she was strong enough to do her job. He was strict about work and reporting to work on time, 5:00 a.m., to the minute. Those who were late, he reported to the police. The police undressed the person and beat him/her until blood ran, while the doctor watched.

Besides working in the factory, Mom searched through garbage, gathering things she could fix with a needle and thread. After cleaning and making the repairs, she would sell the clothing. Mom also would buy things for one price and then sell them for another. I'm thinking she only slept four hours a day. By keeping busy, Mom didn't have time to think of the past. Even without Dad, somehow, she performed miracles with what she accomplished.

We were learning to live a different way. Many times, we wished we were dead. I tried to help Mom. I remember cleaning the dishes, helping in the garden and picking stuff out of the garbage. It was because of Mom that I have such respect for women. At night, in Yiddish, my mother talked to God and asked "why?" I still believe in God. Is there something better to believe in? However, some human beings you can't trust with a ten-foot pole.

One day while working in the market, Mom saw another man wearing Dad's jacket. It had been custom-made with Dad's name on the lining. This man was a former neighbor from Krasnobród,-Lubelski, a Pole, who wasn't Jewish. We believed the only way he could have gotten the jacket was by killing Dad. We thought he must have followed Dad to where he hid things for trading purposes. *Leibl* took care of the murderer after double-checking the lining. This cousin had been working in the underground for Russia's secret police.

In Zhmerinka, I could attend a school. It was a Jewish day school with two orthodox teachers. I remember they had beards and side-locks. They taught us everything, from reading, writing and arithmetic to the history of Palestine and Zionism. I remember those history lessons clearly as those were the only words I wanted to remember from that time. I wanted to bury the memories of the rest of my life. I don't know if I will ever be able to get rid of those memories. Going to this school was a time when I first remember having fun. I became a child at the age of six and a half. Mom thought the Germans had forgotten that they had a few Jews in this ghetto.

By the end of 1943, we learned from within the community that the Germans were retreating. One of the main reasons was the Russian winter. Without proper clothing, they were freezing and couldn't fight. They couldn't perform, period. Another reason was that the Russians were coming. Russian airplanes began to bomb heavily. The Germans appeared to be giving up. Many seemed in a daze like they didn't know what was going on. Some were getting civilian clothing and escaping to neighboring towns. Mom helped load their things onto railroad cars.

By this time, Mom and I were more concerned about the Ukrainian and Romanian guards, than the Germans. These Ukrainian and Romanian guards were also Nazis. We thought they were worse than the Germans. I still remember their yellowish/green uniforms. The Ukrainians wanted to get hold of the personal property; they questioned a lot of people in the ghetto.

We all kept hearing that the Russians were getting closer. The Judenrat came around and warned us to prepare for the worst. Kutzenko had built a crawling space, or cellar, under his home. He could access this space through a wooden door inside his closet. He hid us in his secret space with food and other members of the ghetto including my uncle and aunt. The hiding space was unfinished with sand and stones.

After about ten days of hiding, we heard footsteps nearby. Everyone started praying to God, *Shema Yisrael* (the first two words or title of a special prayer, "Hear Oh Israel"). Then we heard laughter. From such a sound, we knew it was good news; we realized we had been liberated. I was almost seven years old. We heard knocking on the door. Since Nazis would have crashed through the door, we figured it was safe to answer. It was March 22, 1944; we were very lucky to have been liberated while the war was still going on.

Our liberators were short, husky teenage soldiers from Uzbekistan and Kazakstan, countries in central Asia that were republics of the USSR. They also disliked the Ukrainian Nazis more than the German Nazis. They were avenging the raping of their mothers, sisters and daughters. These soldiers (some on horses) were so mad that whenever they saw a Nazi (half dead) or running, they would catch him and then they would cut off a finger to get a ring or a hand to get a watch or bracelet. My uncle was so excited; he grabbed, hugged and kissed one of the soldiers' leaders and brought him inside to offer vodka. For a short while, we continued to live in Kutzenko's home until we were ready to move on.

Uncle Benjamin and Cousin Leibl, in front of the apartment complex, 1980s.

1 "Zhmerinka, " *Encyclopaedia Judaica*, 1971, vol. 16, accessed 17 April 2017, www. encyclopedia.com.
2 *Ibid.*
3 *Ibid.*
4 "Where is…" Google, accessed 22 July 2016, www.au.geotargit.com.

9 RETURN TO POLAND

Although we had been liberated, the war was not over; the armistice would not be signed until May of 1945. Even after the armistice was signed, there were resistance fighters who didn't get the news until September. Not knowing what the Russians would do, (Mom did not trust them), we moved on; it was *Pesach* (Passover) time in 1944. Mom and I took a train back to Poland. We wanted to see if we could find any other relatives. The war was still going on which made us very fearful and uneasy about our living situation. At that time, many Jewish people had returned to Poland and created a kibbutz. A kibbutz is a commune where people live and work together, sharing the rewards. I don't remember where in Poland this kibbutz was located. A group of 40-50 young people organized this kibbutz; many were 18 or 19 years of age. Some of the members were from Mom's town. In fact some were her cousins. Eventually, they wanted to form a kibbutz in Israel.

In Poland, we lived on a kibbutz with other survivors. This photo shows the children. I am not in this picture.

As a group, the kibbutzniks wanted to make sure that the children were safe. I was allowed to play children's games that I had never experienced. I felt like I had been reborn and returned to my once lost childhood. Although I was seven years old, I played patty cake. To the children, such a simple activity was a big thing. For a little over a year, we all lived in this commune, concentrated in a small area as a family. In a big hall, we slept together on beds or on the floor. We grew vegetables and raised cows and chickens. To the outside communities, we sold some of these farm products.

In this kibbutz photo, Mom is in the top row, second from the left, in a flowered dress. I am in the middle of the bottom row, laying down to the far left. Our flag looks like an Israeli flag, before Israel became a state.

Another photo of the children on the kibbutz. I am far left in the first row.

On the kibbutz, I became friends with Ratner. I'm the short one.

10 FLEEING TO CZECHOSLOVAKIA AND THEN AUSTRIA

While living on the kibbutz, we again realized that the Poles wanted to get rid of the Jews. Some Poles even told us they didn't want to do so; they had to. While we saw Polish people killing Jews, we had no way to fight back. The authorities said the killers were drunks and couldn't be blamed. Consequently, we realized we had to leave the kibbutz. Most of the members went to Cyprus, near Greece, and from there, snuck into Palestine. I wanted to go to Palestine because I had made a lot of friends who chose that path. However, for whatever

Before the war, Mom was a member of a youth movement, in training for future life in a Jewish country. In Austria, 1947, I became an automatic member as Mom's son. Mom made everything that I am wearing, except for the scarf. To make the pants, she used an army blanket.

reason, Mom wasn't ready to make such a move. Instead, she chose for us to travel to Czechoslovakia; it was the spring of 1945.

To prepare for our trip, Mom bought a large overcoat for me to wear, and many packs of cigarettes, on the black market. At the time, cigarettes were a hot item; they were not easily available. She hid the cigarettes inside the coat's lining until she was able to sell them. This would be our source of income as we travelled. For more spending money, she used what she had earned by repairing and selling items she found in the trash back in Zhmerinka. Together with a few other families, about 14 of us took trains to Czechoslovakia; it was almost a month before the war ended. In Czechoslovakia, we saw it wasn't safe there either as the country was occupied by the Nazis. So, by walking and taking trains, we crossed the border into Austria and ended up in Staiern, in the American zone's displaced persons camp, run by the military.

In the displaced persons camp, I saw and experienced things I didn't know existed, like chocolate. The camp staff gave us physicals, shots and vaccines. Each family had its own room, our first real room, and nice, clean bunk beds

Mom and me, 1946/1947

Mom 1947

At the displaced persons camp with my new friends, I'm the one without a jacket.

Me, 1947

with as many blankets as we wanted. Mom arranged to get an extra blanket; she used it to make clothing for me, pants and a jacket.

I'll never forget how the leaders of the camp and GIs took all of the kids to a mountain resort, in Strobel, for five days. From the pool, we could look up and see a train traveling through the mountains. We even learned how to swim. That was a memory we all loved and definitely will never forget. It was a nice break for our parents as well.

While living at the displaced persons camp in Austria, the GIs treated us, the children, to a vacation at a lake resort, Strobel. They taught us to swim. I am standing fourth from the right side.

11 ONWARD TO PARIS, FRANCE AND THEN BOLIVIA

In June of 1947, when I was ten, we left the displaced persons camp. We took a train to Paris, through the assistance of a refugee organization called "Joint" or the American Jewish Joint Distribution Committee. For four to five months, we stayed in a Paris hotel with other refugees while we waited for our emigration papers to be finalized. This hotel was located near a subway and the Eifel Tower. I learned my way around so well that I could have been a guide on the metro. Next door to the hotel was a businessman who sold leather goods from a wholesale factory and he could speak Yiddish. I wound up helping him with the delivery of some of his products. Mom went with me the first two or three times and then I sold the leather goods by myself.

Mom had four siblings in the United States. Yet, within a few weeks of arriving in Paris, we learned the United States was not an option. This major setback was due to the United States' immigration policy's strict quota. President Franklin D Roosevelt's immigration policies stunk and the fact that his secretary of state and assistant secretary of state were anti-Semitic, did not help. (President Roosevelt died before the war ended.) I wondered why the United States wouldn't let us in; I thought we did something wrong. Later on, I realized the reason was disguised as political, but really was anti-Semitism.

Mom contacted her brother, in Bolivia. At that time, only two countries were accepting refugees, Bolivia and Cuba. Most of the Jews in Bolivia were from central and eastern Europe.[1] By the late 1940s, the number of Bolivia's Jews peaked at about 10,000.[2] Most of Bolivia's Jews lived in La Paz, the center of the government and where Mom's brother lived.[3]

In November of 1947, we migrated to Bolivia; I was ten years old. We took a ship, the "Compania," from Marseille. On that boat, we slept in clean bunk beds at the lowest level. Almost 90 of us were going to Bolivia as refugees. A good number of the ship's passengers were paying customers, not refugees; they had beds on the upper levels. I don't remember getting seasick. But I do remember becoming friends with a three-year-old girl, Cyra, who I'm still friends with to this day. I treated her like a little sister. She was born in Uzbekistan and her parents were from Poland. There were locked gates between the boat's levels. I remember as kids how we tried to sneak up to the upper levels, just for fun. Sometimes, we succeeded. This worried our parents; they were concerned for our safety, of course.

1 "Bolivia, The Jewish Community," International Jewish Cemetery Project, International Association of Jewish Genealogical Societies, accessed 5 July 2016, www. iajgsjewishcemeteriyproject.org
2 Ibid.
3 Ibid.

MY YEARS IN BOLIVIA

We left Marseille during the third week of October in 1947. First our boat stopped at a port in Morocco, Africa where we spent two full days in the harbor. Then we travelled back to Marseille before sailing onto South America. We landed in Rio de Janeiro, Brazil on November 5th and were welcomed by representatives from a Jewish organization; they hugged and cried with us. We stayed there for one week, adjusting to the climate. Again, we stayed in a hotel. Then a bunch of us were put on a plane to La Paz, Bolivia where we landed on Nov. 13th. Again, some community leaders came to welcome us with my uncle and a few of his friends. Back then, the population of La Paz was much smaller, about 350,000 and the number of Jews totaled 5,000. La Paz was beautiful! I would very much like to go back to visit, but health concerns keep me away (altitude).

In Bolivia, we passed the required medical exams. We didn't have as many medical issues as other survivors. I credit my health to the fact that I was never a big eater. So, I was better able to get by on less food. It wasn't until years later that I learned of my minor medical problems related to my Holocaust experiences, problems such as calcium deficiency. However, Mom was malnourished and suffered from more health problems.

Upon our arrival, we moved in with my Uncle *Moishe Yosl*, into his two-bedroom apartment. I shared a bedroom with Mom. We lived in the upper apartment and had our own balcony; it was shaped like a semi-circle. There was a park across the street where I played ball with kids from the neighborhood. Most of my playmates were not Jewish. It was a third world country, yet the neighborhood was very clean; you wouldn't see dog poop lying around. Our neighbors were nice, innocent, down-to-earth people. They became our truly good friends. We had keys to some of our neighbors' homes. I adjusted by playing with the neighborhood kids. Over time, the German population grew considerably, and not the ones we wanted. However, most Nazis escaped to Argentina where the president was a Nazi Party member. (Argentina helped to hide the big time Nazi murderers.)

We joined a synagogue right away. There were three synagogues. Ours was extremely orthodox. Another was very conservative and a third was more liberal. We followed orthodox traditions. As a boy in La Paz, I attended religious school, three days a week, and learned the holy books. This was additional to public school which I attended five to five and a half days per week.

When we first came to Bolivia, I didn't know any Spanish. I started school in February and dealt with the language barriers for six or seven months. Despite my age, I was put in second grade while I worked on my language skills. By June, I was fluent in Spanish. I did well in school, but socially I wasn't very friendly. I had psychological problems due to my childhood experiences and was treated by a local psychiatrist who wasn't able to help me, initially. He wasn't able to diagnose my overall state of mind. I was one of his very few Holocaust survivor patients. Neither could he do much to help Mom. At the time, I didn't want to be with other kids, unlike in Europe where I did fine with others my age. I didn't want to open up. I had a hard time trusting people. I was forced to be very mature for my age. There was a difference in age among the Holocaust survivors who were children. Unlike many, I was old enough to remember. At first, language was a barrier, but even when I could understand and speak Spanish, I drove the doctor crazy. However, in time, he became a big help to me. After a few years, I felt more comfortable socially, more adjusted.

Mom and I designed this Jewish New Year's greeting card while we lived in Bolivia, when I was twelve. We sent it to all our relatives and friends.

About two years after moving to Bolivia, we moved to a three-bedroom apartment. The two-bedroom apartment had become a little tight. Furthermore, the landlord kept raising the rent every few months. On the floor beneath us lived a family with twins, red heads who were about eight years younger than me. I remember how they used to get in trouble blaming each other. They weren't there long. Like other families, they eventually moved to Israel.

In Bolivia, I made many friends from Maccabi. This is a birthday party for a friend. I am about 13 years old and standing in the top right corner.

Mom didn't want to leave her brother, *Moishe Yosl* out of a sense of responsibility, she felt we owed him our support.

My uncle worked as a peddler; he began this job when he first came to Bolivia in 1939. In May of 1948, I started helping him by collecting money from his customers. Mom kept busy; she worked as my uncle's bookkeeper, in addition to cooking, cleaning and sewing our clothing. Although my uncle had developed a good business, Mom suggested that he switch to money lending and make life easier for himself. By the end of 1949, he gradually began to make the transition.

There were six grades in the primary school and six grades in the high school. From second grade, I jumped to fourth grade, and then skipped another year. Mom encouraged me to read. When I was eleven years old, I tested Mom's directions by buying a sex magazine and read it so she could see the cover. As she walked by, she said "You're reading, good!" In college, I can remember reading three to five books a week, in Yiddish, Spanish or English. But as I always say, that was then; now I read whenever I get a chance. But I do read newspapers ("Democrat & Chronicle", "Jewish Ledger", "Forward", and optical journals) and I do try to read regular stuff when I am in the mood.

While we lived in Bolivia, we experienced the government's instability through observing uprisings. One particularly memorable day was April 9, 1952 when people were fighting in the streets. What was quite interesting to me was the number of bullets that landed on our apartment's closed in balcony. Somehow, I wasn't hurt; neither was I really scared.

By the end of 1953, my uncle was no longer a peddler. By that point, I assisted as his bookkeeper. In fact, Mom and I took over much of his money-lending business. This uncle was not a happy man, having lost his wife and daughter back in Poland. He cried a lot. Although he never forgave Poland and Germany, he blamed himself more. Although Mom offered good business advice, my uncle didn't always listen to her because of conflicting advice from his close friends. One such friend helped him to lose over $250,000 (United States dollars). Even at the age of eleven, I knew that friend was no good, but Mom told me not to say anything.

By the time I entered secondary school, I caught up academically with my age group. Starting in seventh grade, we took 14 subjects at one time. The day began at 8:00, at 1:00, we went home for lunch. Classes began again at 2:30 and ended at 4:30 or 5:00. In high school, I really started getting involved, socially in the Jewish community. Through the community, I met Israeli Cultural Ambassadors. They taught us about the kibbutzim, Israeli songs and dances. I became a Jew. Given the fact of what we went through before Bolivia, I felt at times that I did not want to be Jewish. These feelings changed once we moved to Bolivia. In fact, I thought at one point, if you weren't Jewish, you weren't good. Mom straightened me out and taught me to be respectful of other's beliefs.

By ninth grade, I started getting involved with athletics and a Jewish athletics organization, Maccabi. Most of the members were survivors or second-generation survivors. We wanted to be as good if not better than everyone else. The Israeli Cultural Ambassadors helped us; they encouraged us to believe in ourselves and have a strong sense of self-worth. However, at a young age, I also learned the importance of knowing how to lose. My gym teachers spent considerable effort emphasizing that winning is not the entire objective. I also got involved in local sports and ended up in amateur leagues for soccer, basketball and track & field. The one hundred meter dash was my race. Although I did my best for my basketball team, I wasn't that good. Soccer was my better sport.

I played soccer in La Paz, Bolivia for eight years, in high school and Maccabi. I am in the top row to the far left.

Not only did I play sports, but I helped organize them as well. I became a director of the board. As a board member, to represent Maccabi, I attended Jewish Federation meetings. A lot of Bolivia's sports facilities were built with Jewish money. We did all this to show our appreciation for all the country had done for us. Most of Maccabi's Jews were of German descent as most Jews of Polish descent went to Israel. I remembered that when living in Poland, I often heard Jews talking about Palestine, not Bolivia.

Also in high school, I became involved in Yiddish theater. I liked the plays by Sholom Aleichem. In particular, I remember one of his plays, "Hitting the Jackpot" ("*Dus Groise Gevinst*") where I was one of the Rabbis. Acting did not come easy for me. I had to study very hard to learn my lines. This affected my grades, but just temporarily, so Mom didn't mind. The plays were performed for two weeks, three times a week.

Uncle *Moishe Yosl's* business had developed well with Mom's guidance, but eventually, my uncle made some very bad decisions. As a result, I decided to take some night courses, in 1955, while earning extra money during the day. I graduated with my classmates, the following year, 1956, as a day student.

As a high school student, I liked physics. Due to our limited finances, I realized that I couldn't afford to pursue a higher education. Consequently, I chose a career that wouldn't require an advanced degree yet would involve physics, opticianry. One month after graduating from high school at the age of nineteen, I arranged to work as an apprentice at a Jewish optical shop, Optica La-Paz. I had met this store's owner through his involvement with the Jewish community's sports activities. He had high expectations of me, more than the other apprentices. At first this upset me until Mom explained it was a compliment; the owner recognized my

I graduated from high school in 1956, and am being presented with my diploma by the acting vice principal.

potential. My first task was to sweep the floor. Eventually, I learned how to grind lenses by hand rather than rely on a machine. I kept this position for almost four years.

Standing in the top row, far left, I am the youngest member of the board of directors for one of the oldest soccer clubs in La Paz, Bolivia. It is called "Bolivar" named after Simon Bolivar who was the liberator of Bolivia, Peru, Ecuador, Colombia and Venezuela, early 1800s. The trophy is for a local championship.

*My friend Cyra and I have had a long friendship.
We first became friends on the boat to Bolivia
and are still friends today.*

1963, I am participating in a bowling tournament in La Paz, Bolivia for Maccabi.

13 LIVING IN THE UNITED STATES

A college degree was very important to Mom, probably more important to her than to me. A good education is important to Jewish parents, because of our past. After Mom remarried in 1955, I felt more comfortable with the idea of leaving her to pursue a degree in the United States. When I was 23 years old (in 1960), I left to study opticianry at Erie Community College in Buffalo, New York. I chose Erie Community College because it was close to my relatives in New York City and New Jersey. I thought I might be able to visit with them. However, they were too busy. While in college, I connected with some of these relatives. I probably should have insisted on getting together. Although I already had an opticianry background from Bolivia, I needed the required certification from the United States. My American education didn't teach me much more than I had already learned in Bolivia. Nevertheless, it did help me to improve my English, and of course I got my diploma which I hung above Mom's bed when I went back to Bolivia.

While attending college, I worked as an optician as I already had four years of an apprenticeship back in Boliva. My income, together with financial support from my stepfather supported my living expenses and education. Besides working as an optician, I gave lectures to Buffalo high school students about Bolivia and South America. Additionally, I worked as a waiter, and for three weeks, I even cleaned toilets at a steel mill in Lackawanna, south of Buffalo. During my second year, I bought a 1955 two door DeSoto. I even began to drive on the Sabbath, which I never did in Bolivia. My first apartment,

Enjoying La Paz with my friends; I'm second from the left.

Summertime, 1963, at an automobile/swim club in La Paz, Bolivia. These are my childhood friends. I am standing in the back row, to the right, wearing sunglasses. Gabriela is sitting in the center of the front row.

I found with the assistance of the Jewish Federation in Buffalo. I was within walking distance of the synagogue that I occasionally attended. I also attended Hillel services across the street from the University of Buffalo on Main and Kenmore Streets.

Living in Buffalo, I saw things I couldn't do in Bolivia. I could express myself without worrying about censorship. I didn't have to worry about what bad things could happen as I had experienced in Europe. After graduating, I returned to Bolivia in 1963. I wasn't yet ready to become a United States resident. I wasn't sure where I wanted to live. My initial plan was to go to the United States just for college. I never planned for my future, just for tomorrow. I've always found it impossible to see beyond the next couple years. Maybe it's because of my survival upbringing. There was a time when we couldn't even plan day to day. Why not plan for less and end up doing more?

When I returned to Bolivia, I didn't work as an optician. Instead, I managed a textile business. At that time, I began to date Gabriela Berkowitz who I had met through my Maccabi activities. She was born in Bolivia but her parents were from Germany. They had emigrated to Bolivia in 1939. Unlike me, she went to a Jewish Day School.

Gabriela's high school yearbook photograph

Gabriela, my bride

On November 4, 1967, I married Gabriela. We left La Paz on November 8th for our honeymoon, visiting Peru, Ecuador, Colombia, Panama, Miami, Florida and New York, New York on our way to our new home in Rochester, New York. We chose Rochester because Gabriela had a sister who lived there. She married a lawyer, from Long Island, who specialized in international law. At the time, he was employed by Alliance for Progress which was started by John F Kennedy. They started dating while he was working in La Paz, Bolivia and eventually married there. After working for the government for a few years, he was hired by Xerox and that is how they ended up in Rochester, New York. I wanted to be in that area because Rochester was known as the optical center of the world.

Upon arriving in Rochester, we moved into a one-bedroom apartment and I started my career in the United States as an optician. Five months later, we moved into a two-bedroom at a new apartment complex. Gabriela was pregnant at the time and a few months later, we had our first child, Joseph whom we named after Dad.

Gabriela's parents sitting between my stepdad and Mom at the wedding of one of our friends, May 31, 1969

Since I had kept up with some of my college friends, we immediately had a group of friends, in addition to near-by relatives. We joined Temple Beth El and both became members of B'nai Brith. Similarly, we eventually both joined bowling leagues. In 1971, we had a daughter, Brenda Rachel, whom we named after Mom's mother (*Baile Ruchel*). By the summer of 1972, we bought our own home in a suburb of Rochester, Brighton. My son and daughter had a very close relationship to each other and they both did well in school. Both of them also played soccer.

Joseph now lives in Steamboat Springs, Colorado where he has a career in property management. He married and has two children, one of whom he named after my brother, *Naftuli* (Nathan). He is very bright and very good in sports, like his dad. Zanah is three years younger. Although she's only a little girl, I can already sense her strong individuality as well as the strong sibling bonds. Brenda now lives in Rockland County, New York, with a career in retail management. My son and daughter never learned the full extent of my experiences. As a parent, such a conversation is extremely difficult.

By the mid 1970s, Gabriela's parents moved to Miami Beach, Florida. Once a year, we began to visit Gabriela's parents and some other friends. Mom moved to the United States in 1991; she was 79 years old. Until then, she was very happy in Bolivia. However, I became concerned that her friends and friends' families were no longer there for her. I wanted her to live closer to us. By the time Mom moved here, my stepfather, uncles and aunts had already passed away.

Mom is sitting in her room at the Jewish Home. It is her 80th birthday.

Mom lived with us for about five months. In February of 1992, she moved into the Jewish Home of Rochester. Mom never complained about food because she didn't have it during the war. Like Mom, I am always thankful for food. People need to show more appreciation for what they have and stop the feeling of entitlement. I visited Mom at the nursing home often. To my surprise, some of those people hadn't seen their children in two years or longer. Mom died in 2005 when she was three weeks shy of her 93rd birthday. Since her passing, I visit her gravesite as often as I can.

Gabriela and I with our children in Steamboat Springs, Colorado, after we took a balloon ride, around July 1995.

My son and daughter, visiting Mom at the Jewish Home. Mom is 90 years old.

Gabriela and I with our children, summer 2013, our home, Rochester, New York.

Out of my relatives in the United States, I contacted several who were never able to get together with me. In the United States, everybody is busy and there is not enough time for family, unlike in Europe or South America where family is first. When I first arrived in the United States, I stayed with Uncle Ben for about a week. Out of my relatives, I occasionally would meet with Aunts *Gitl, Male* and Ida (Mom's sister-in-law). I am still in touch with Esther (Uncle *Itzke* and Aunt Ida's daughter).

Pictures of my son, Joseph, and my grandchildren, Nathan and Zanah, in Steamboat Springs, Colorado, November 2016.

14 PRESENTATIONS TO STUDENTS

For about twenty years, I've been giving presentations about the Holocaust in many school districts and various venues throughout New York State. When speaking in Steam Boat Springs, back in 2014, I gave three presentations in one day. I was running on adrenaline. I've spoken to a variety of audiences ranging from sixth graders to college students, senior groups and many others. Most of my presentations are during the spring; I average about ten per year.

At first, I was very scared, but not any more. I do not prepare for these presentations; I just get up and talk. Though the night before is always difficult, bracing myself for vocally reliving the past. I speak freely, explaining my experiences as a boy in the Holocaust. I speak about not having food, not have a bed, not knowing what's going to happen to my family and not knowing what is going to happen in general. Without props, I give the audience good eye contact. Using my hands to help express my feelings, and using body movement throughout the room, I keep the audience alert. To create a positive environment, I assure the students, "It's OK to not know, but it's important to learn. Not knowing is not a crime. That's why you're here." Throughout my presentations, I try to impress upon the children the importance of several basic values: The value of education, hard work, honesty, and overall respect for others. By sharing my experiences with others in the community, I believe I can help people understand the importance of awareness.

Repeatedly, I speak about the need to read as much as they can. "Read about what's happening in the world. Get the facts. Don't just read the sensationalist papers. Knowledge is in reading, not texting." I share how Mom asked me to promise to read as much as I could. Similarly, I keep emphasizing the very special relationship between Mom and me. To me, Mom was everything. Sharing what happened to me helps the students better understand my feelings. I encourage them to also value their family relationships as well as their childhood. Childhood is precious. I didn't have one. My son and daughter love it when I still treat them as

With the cooperation of the Center for Holocaust Awareness and the Jewish Community Federation of Rochester, two survivors of the Holocaust were invited to speak to students in the Global Studies classes at Palmyra-Macedon High School. The talk was arranged by the Social Studies Department and coordinated by teacher **Kristine Lester**.

Alec Mutz and **Samuel Rind** spoke to tenth grade students in two presentations. Mr. Rind, originally from Poland, was a small child during the Holocaust years. All of his relatives except his mother were killed.

"I heard Mr. Rind talk about his experiences as a child," said **Jim Cunningham**, a Pal-Mac junior. "I've read about the Holocaust in books a hundred times, but hearing someone who lived through it talk about it is a whole lot different. We live in a time and place where it's easy to take things for granted. Hearing someone talk about appreciating the right to live is almost impossible for us to understand."

"Mr. Rind gave a good speech on the history of his life," said Pal-Mac sophomore **Eric Phillips**. "He presented his report to a group of 100-120 tenth graders. He told them how he lived in camps and told how his father disappeared one night and his brother was murdered by a German soldier. Even after Mr. Rind escaped captivity, his life didn't get much better. I now think I have a better understanding of the kind of persecution the Jews faced."

"I found the lecture extremely interesting," said Pal-Mac junior **Bethany LeMoyne**. "In class, there are some things that are not taught, and hearing a first-hand experience teaches them. Also, it makes a teenager see the real experienced happenings instead of just trying to imagine hypotheticals; therefore it seems more realistic. He did a great job and kept everyone's interest."

Samuel Rind is pictured with Pal-Mac students (from left) Katie Contino, Jim Cunningham, and Eric Phillips.

I have been speaking to local classrooms for the past 20 years. Through sharing my own experiences, I have been teaching students about the Holocaust. This presentation dates back to 1997.

children and they're in their forties. That's why we're still very close. My wife and I are very rich, not financially, but with our family.

Equally important, I speak of appreciating the beauty of diversity. I tell the students to "look at the variety of people in the classroom, beautiful! This is the way it should be; we get along. Diverse is what every place on earth should be."

I also speak about not wasting food. I tell them "When I see people throw food away, I want to scream. Save it. Go find a homeless or poor person. Being rich doesn't mean you have to be wasteful."

Never have I had a problem with capturing their attention. Using my sense of humor, and my sincere wishes for helping them learn, I believe I provide a positive learning environment. Little do they know, however, how mentally drained I feel upon completing our time together.

Everyone appreciated my efforts. More significantly, I believe I touched their hearts and souls, enlightening them with a deeper understanding of history. For a few examples of the teachers' testimonials, see Appendix A.

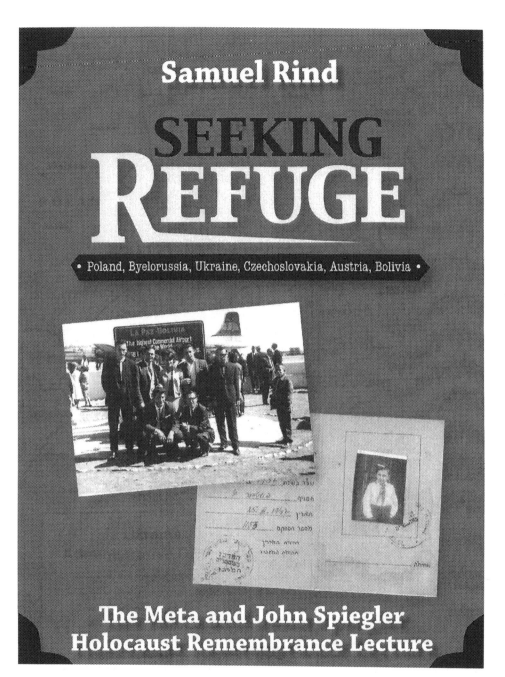

This is the program cover for my presentation at the Corning Museum of Glass, in Corning, New York, April 28, 2014. I also provided this presentation at Steamboat Springs High School, in Steamboat Springs, Colorado, May 9, 2014

GUIDE TO POLAND

In addition to the presentations, in 2013, and again in 2015, I was a participant in an American/Israeli youth program called "Journey for Identity." The program included 16 students from different high schools in the Rochester area and 16 students from Modi'in, Israel (sister city). There were three chaperones besides me: two Israeli chaperones and in 2013, Keith Greer, chairman of the program and in 2015, Richard Gordon, the Coordinator of Teen Education and Israel Trips from the Jewish Federation of Greater Rochester.

According to Richard Gordon, *"The goals of Journey for Identity are regularly revised and updated. A summary of the goals as described for the 2015 trip would include:*

- *Strengthen Jewish pride through learning about the resilience, heroism, and resistance of European Jewry*
- *Deepening of interpersonal ties among youth, and strengthening of ties between the communities*
- *Strengthening of Jewish identity, and increased knowledge of Jewish and American Jewish history in general, and of the Holocaust*
- *Strengthening of the youth's identification with Diaspora Jewry*
- *Creation of an emotional hands-on experience that brings the youth together in the recognition of their common Jewish destiny."*

Before touring Poland, the local teens and those from Israel, spent a week together in Rochester. I participated in some of the events to get acquainted and to share my Holocaust experience. In Poland, we had two tour guides: Nick and Noam (in 2015). Nick, from Poland, spoke about the communities and places; he described how they changed over time. Noam, from Israel's Yad Vashem, Israel's Holocaust Remembrance Center, was the main guide. He spoke about each location's history before and during the Holocaust. As the only Holocaust survivor on the trip, I shared my perspective and experiences. According to Richard, *"It's really Sam who made the experience more personalized. It's with his help that the teens truly gained a sense of the FEEL of the horrors of the Holocaust – way beyond the numbers and facts which are also vitally important."*

In addition to the chaperones, we were always accompanied by Israeli security as required by Israel. The agents always checked all locations before we could enter. I was unable to return to my town of birth, Krasnobród-Lubelski; there wasn't enough time. However, we did visit Mom's town, Józefów-Bilgorajski.

Through these tours, I met Polish citizens who helped with our trips. In 2013, while I was traveling through Poland, I met a woman, in her nineties. The Jewish Holocaust Society recognized her for hiding Jews in her basement. These tours were a most enlightening experience for me as they helped me to distinguish between some present day Poles and those of the past.

By accompanying the teens through Poland, I've changed. Those students have no idea how much they've helped to make my life easier. I learned they were interested in becoming our voices in the future. Although I went to Poland with a very heavy heart, I came back feeling much better. I'm still in touch with most of those kids. I even occasionally meet them in a restaurant. While sitting in the Jewish Community Center's café, I often see their parents. It's nice to hear them comment upon the impressions I've made. One such parent, Seth Silver said *"Sam's humanity was indispensible to the trip: His personal recollection, his ability to relate to the teenagers, as a teen at heart, his ability to be serious when the time was right, to be their guide for the story of the Holocaust, their friend, their teacher. And they loved him."*

Keith Greer, the Chairman of Federation's Journey for Identity Program, provided another perspective of my role as the teen's guide.

"In 2013, I had the opportunity to not only chair the Journey for Identity Program, but to also be the chaperone from Rochester that accompanied the teens on this very unique cultural program. Having worked as a School Social Worker of almost 30 years, I have had the opportunity to work with many wonderful groups of young adults. But this group proved to be extraordinary!! Immensely warm and outgoing, intelligent and insightful, engaging and thoughtful, this group of 32 American and Israeli teens took Sam into their hearts and allowed Sam to do the same with them.

Witnessing Sam's return to his homeland and hearing first hand on his experiences in the Holocaust had a huge impact upon the teens. I had this sense throughout our time in Poland, that for the teens, walking this journey with Sam was akin to taking a trip to a Revolutionary War site and having George Washington as their tour guide. Sam's personal experiences and memories brought this history alive and added a layer of context that would not be available from anyone other than someone who lived in that time.

Prior to this trip, I was involved in the orientation sessions for the Rochester teens and this is where I first met Sam. During one of these sessions, Sam shared his Holocaust testimony with the teens and their parents. At the conclusion of Sam's talk, I found myself worried. It was clear from several pointed remarks made during his presentation, that Sam continued to harbor strong feelings of anger toward the Polish people. Now it is not my place, nor the place of any human being, to in any way judge the feelings of a Holocaust Survivor. But the upcoming trip placed in my hands the responsibility of helping 32 young adults negotiate their own journey of Holocaust learning and I did feel a level of concern about how Sam's anger might impact some of the teens. My concerns proved unfounded!

Once in Poland, this phenomenal group of young adults had a monumental impact on Sam. They listened to his testimony, they cared for him. They witnessed and honored his pain and loss. I believe with all of my heart that every single one of the 32 members of Journey for Identity (2013), played an intimate role in Sam's healing from the moment he stepped off the plane onto Polish soil. Through our experiences together in Poland, we observed Sam lay his anger to rest. The young adults, along with our particularly warm and caring Polish guide who was on the bus with us all week, cried and grieved with Sam and through this process, helped Sam be able to leave Poland with a greater sense of inner peace.

Since the trip, Sam and I have remained good friends. We continue to enjoy attending Buffalo Bills football games together."

Through numerous letters in "Thank You Books," each of the teens expressed how my presence affected their experience. For a few examples of their letters, see Appendix B.

16 MY CONCLUDING THOUGHTS

At my school presentations, I have sometimes said "Even though my words may seem resentful or hateful, who am I to forgive? If the six million will forgive, I will." I just want everyone to pay attention to the world around them. We shouldn't take people for granted. We shouldn't believe it can't happen here in the United States. That's exactly what people said in Germany. We can only stop it from happening by being aware of what's going on around us.

Although I live in the United States, I still have fears of anti-Semitism. Recently, I observed how the United Nations declared Israel to be the country with the worst women's rights policies. How can they possibly suggest such a wildly inaccurate idea?! I have very strong feelings for Israel. Consequently, I am very aware of negative comments. How can Americans, especially Jewish Americans suggest that the Israeli government should give back the land without conflicting with a historically strong parallel? The United States never gave back the land to the Native Americans or Mexico.

We must be aware of genocides happening right now. We must be aware of millions of people being killed because they have the wrong look or the wrong religion. The worst of it all is too many people seem to be aware but simply don't care. I have had occasions where people have told me up front that I live in the United States now and I should be more concerned about the United States than the rest of the world. Specifically, I was told to worry more about the United States than I am worrying about Israel. As a Jewish Holocaust survivor, how can I do that?!

I would like to live forever to teach human beings about the Holocaust, to teach everyone to not let it happen again.

MEDITATION IN MOM'S MEMORY

"Though we are separated, dear mother, in this solemn hour, I call to mind the love and solicitude with which you tended and watched over my childhood, ever mindful of my welfare, and ever anxious for my happiness. Many were the sacrifices you made to ennoble my heart and instruct my mind. What I achieved is because of your influence and what I am, I have become through you. Though you are no longer physically present, the lessons that you imparted unto me shall ever remain with me.

If at times, I have failed in showing you the love and appreciation, which you so worthily deserved, if I have been thoughtless and ungrateful; I ask to be forgiven. I pray that your spirit inspires me to noble and intelligent living, so that when my days on earth are ended, and I arrive at the Throne of Mercy, I shall be deemed worthy of you, and to be reunited with you in God. Amen."

"Book of Remembrance, 2016-2017/5777," page 6, adapted from the memorial service, 10/12/16, of Temple Beth El, 139 Winton Road, Rochester, NY.

APPENDIX A, TESTIMONIALS

Stacy Cougle, a teacher in the Churchville-Chili School District, wrote:

Sam Rind visited our 6th grade self-contained Special Education class at Churchville-Chili Middle School. The students in this class have moderate learning disabilities and other social emotional challenges. We prepared the students for his visit by reading his short biography that Bonnie sent and creating questions to ask. The students had previously read the novel, "Number The Stars," and we did a mini-unit on the Holocaust. Due to the sensitive nature of this dark period in history and the nature of our students, we took care in selecting and presenting the content to our students. After this unit, the students were beginning a non-fiction narrative writing unit that required them to learn about people who have overcome adversity and through perseverance, endured and thrived. Another goal of that unit was to develop empathy through their emotional journey. Therefore, Sam's visit would be the perfect learning opportunity for our students to address both units of study.

During Sam's visit, he spoke to our students about his experiences living through the Holocaust. I was so relieved to discover that Sam was very comfortable speaking to our group of special needs students. I was uncertain as to how our students would react (even though I felt that we had adequately prepared them). However, Sam was wonderful in establishing a rapport with the students during such a short period of time. He asked each student to introduce him/herself to him. During this time he made small talk with each of them which made each student feel special and recognized. He mentioned that he has a son named Joey and there was a Joey in the class who was a bit of a handful. He made the comment that "Joey is a name for troublemakers I know this because I have a son named Joey and he is a troublemaker!" Our Joey thought it was hysterical and so did we! Sam was very insightful and related very well to our students from the moment he walked into the room wearing his Buffalo Bills baseball cap and shared common experiences about his childhood.

Sam began telling about the beginning of the Holocaust and Hitler's rise to power. He shared that life became very difficult for his family and his parents realized that it was no longer safe to stay in Poland. He had a very big family and they decided to split up, rather than stay together during their journey to a safer place. They felt it would increase their chances of survival. Sam told of his lengthy time living in camps, their unsanitary living conditions, the scarcity of food, and the hard labor he was forced to do. His father's role in looking after his family and always putting them first was a central focus of his story. The students were appalled to hear that his father exchanged a 18 carat gold ring for ONE potato. Furthermore, when Sam shared how they used the one potato to feed four people, the students were in greater disbelief. Later, when Sam revealed his father was killed for his leather jacket, there were many tear-filled eyes. Sam explained that at 5 years of age, he lost his childhood and became the "man of the house." He took a little detour at this point to impress upon the students the importance of enjoying their childhood. He reinforced the necessity to play and be happy, to enjoy life.

However, the most shocking piece of his life story that hit home for many of our students, who have been touched by the death of their classmate who passed away last year from cancer, was the senseless and violent death of Sam's baby brother. The emotional response from the students was overwhelming. Silence. You could hear a pin drop. As much as they were prepared to hear of rampant death and the incomprehensible treatment of humans, they were not prepared for this. The fact that the atrocities of the Holocaust did not discriminate against age, really impacted my students. I've been teaching this content for 22 years and each year I am amazed by the number of students who make this realization during our studies. Learning that 1.25 million children lost their lives, their childhood, was a difficult life lesson for them to learn. Sam's story made this very real for them.

Another part of Sam's experience that we were enamored by was the intelligence and foresight of his mother. Her intuition on how to survive this devastating experience was remarkable. Sam's infinite amount of gratitude and love for his mother permeated his stories and was reflected in his wavering voice and gentle eyes. He said that he "owed his mother everything" and she was the smartest person in the world. The indomitable bond between Sam and his mother clearly kept them both alive. Sam ended this section of his talk by telling the students to be grateful for their parents and to respect all they do for them.

Sam infused many of these life lessons into his visit. He concluded his visit by telling the students that THEY CAN MAKE A DIFFERENCE! They have the opportunity, as a generation, to make an impact on the way history plays out. He noted that this type of discrimination and acts of inhumanity still happen today. It is up to them to stop the hate, stop the violence, and create a more tolerant and compassionate generation.

I am so appreciative that my students had this opportunity to meet and speak with Sam. His story made history come alive for them. Our youth live in a 'virtual' world where it is sometimes hard to determine fantasy from reality. It is critical that history does not remain on the page of a textbook where it is left alone to be forgotten. Sam brought his experience of living through the Holocaust off the page and made it a living, breathing experience for my students.

Sam's visit left an indelible impression on my students. The days that followed were filled with reflections about Sam's remarkable courage and strength to press on in the face of oppression and adversity, at such a young age. From their comments, it was evident that the students had developed a great sense of empathy through this experience. Of course, through this reflection they generated more questions that they wished they had asked! The experience of being this close to a piece of history that is fading, with the imminent passing of Holocaust survivors, is something that our younger generations will only encounter through the written documentation or videos. Sam Rind is a gift to our children who need to know about the Holocaust, who need to remember to show tolerance, and who have the chance to make the world a better place.

Tara DeVay, a teacher in the Geneseo Central School District, wrote:

"I have had Sam come and speak to my classes now for five years and each experience has been different. He tells his story in a very unique way imparting wisdom to the students along the way. By this I mean he has yet to tell his story from start to finish...he loops around and as he comes to certain parts he gives advice to the students. Always he is reminding them to respect their parents...especially their mothers because they are smarter and they "know what you are up to". He tells the kids that education is the key to being successful and shares his educational background focusing on how he reads several books a week and how it was his mother that taught him.

He also motivates the kids to do something about current human rights violations. He does his best to try and impart what he has learned throughout his life to the students when he speaks to them. Currently, I have a group of students who saw him speak and were motivated to go and do something about human rights violations that are occurring today. These students went out on their own and raised money for the Child Soldiers of Uganda and Burma children who have also experienced violence. They pushed me to form an extracurricular club we have named "The Do Gooders". This group is working to bring awareness to current/recent human rights violations and will be raising money to assist others in need. I have another student who came to me at the end of this past school year and she and I worked to bring in a Lost Boy from Sudan to speak to the student body. Through fundraising we were able to donate over $800 to his organization, Building Minds in South Sudan. All of this began because she was so moved by what Sam and other survivors that speak to kids do."

Joe Tobia, the former principal of the All Saints Academy, wrote a letter in his school's spring newsletter in 2014, complimenting my presentation to his students.

Our 7th and 8th grade students recently had a visitor. The stories shared by Mr. Samuel Rind, a Holocaust Survivor, deeply touched our young people with a desire to work for justice in our world. For, even as we advance as a civilization, the deep seeded plague of ethnic and racial bigotry continues to damage our world.

Mr. Rind spoke at the school following his presentation at the Meta and John Speigler Holocaust Remembrance Lecture held on Monday, April 28 at the Corning Museum of Glass.

Sam Rind's father was killed for his leather jacket. His brother was beaten to death on their mother's lap. And his aunt was executed while her two daughters stood behind her. The Polish-born Holocaust-survivor lived in numerous ghettos and concentration camps as a child before finally escaping to freedom.

He told the students that he wanted people to use the memory of the Holocaust to prevent other genocides around the world.

"We must learn from the past. I want you to be aware that history repeats itself if we do nothing," Mr. Rind said. "The Holocaust is not a Jewish thing," he said, noting that Gypsies, homosexuals and other groups were also targeted by the Nazis."

Respect for others is key to the special environment that our teachers and staff work to create at All Saints Academy. As a faith-based, value-centered school, we strive to bring the Gospel message of God's universal love for His creation into practice.

The executive director of the Southern Tier Central Regional Planning Board, Marcia Weber, similarly expressed her feelings about the importance of my presentations to the community. Following my lecture at the Corning Museum of Glass, in May of 2014, she sent me the following message:

I was one of the people at the dinner and at your presentation in Corning on April 28, and I've been meaning to write to tell you how meaningful and important your visit was. So many people have told me that they were very moved by your story, and I know that there were many who had not heard such a story first-hand before that night. Everyone said how grateful they were that you shared your history with them, and they recognized that it must have been difficult for you to do so. I understand your visits to the classrooms were great and that the kids really responded to you. This connection is just what is needed to make the Holocaust real to the next generation. They will remember what you said!

I enjoyed talking with you before and after the presentation, and I hope we have an opportunity to meet again. The committee that planned the lecture and the whole community thank you for coming to Corning to share your past with us and explain why we must be vigilant to prevent future horrors.

Thank you so much!

APPENDIX B, TEENS' TESTIMONIALS

Dear Sam,

Thank you. Those two short words almost don't seem like enough to express how much your presence on this trip meant to me and every other kid on this bus. Visiting many of the sites we did, it was difficult to imagine what went on there both before and during the Holocaust. Your stories and memories helped make Noam's stories feel as real as I know they were. Hearing about such monstrosities can prove almost impossible because my first hand knowledge up to this point has been that the world is a good place to live. I've learned and heard about terrible things all over the world throughout human history, but until hearing survivors speak it all seemed so distant. I'm sure it's hard to go back to some of those memories, but I also know that you're fully aware of how important it is. I hope this trip has helped you too. Don't forget how much you mean to so many people.

Love,
Rachel Cardiel

Dear Sam,

The impact your ideas have made on me is unbelievable. You made this trip extremely meaningful for me and helped me make Poland a spiritual experience. But I think your best quality is your ability to rejuvenate and make a room light up. You became our friend in addition to a teacher. You made us both laugh and cry and I can't thank you enough. You make me proud to be Jewish.

Thank you,
Ben Richardson

Dear Sam,

You are such an amazing person and you make me proud to be Jewish. It takes so much courage to tell your story. I also really like the style you tell the stories. I will continue to pass on your story along with the many others we heard. I'm honored to be with you and amazed how you keep such a positive, funny attitude. I hope to see you in the Rochester area once I get home. I will value family so much more and can't wait to hold them close (because it's not the same on the phone). The relationship you had/have with your mom is beautiful. Having you on this journey has made it even more special. THANK YOU!

Love,
Sarah Krieger

Sarah and me on the tour bus in Poland, July 2013.

Dear Sam,

I have had an amazing experience traveling with you through Poland. Your presence on this trip has added a unique and unforgettable dimension. I wanted to let you know that I think it was incredibly courageous of you to return to such a horrendous place, as well as noble to help educate the future generations so that such an event can never happen again. Thank you so much for sharing your story with our group and I promise we will never forget. It is now up to us to pass down the stories and the experience to our children and grandchildren. Please know that you have been a key component in this process and I will tell your story to my future children. I greatly enjoyed the long conversation we had on the airplane and your advice about well-roundedness was greatly appreciated. If you ever need or want to talk about this experience (or the Buffalo Sabres), please feel free to call me anytime.

Thank you for an amazing experience,
Daniel Silver

In addition to the thank you letters, one of the teens submitted a testimonial for the purpose of my memoir. Lior Burg from Israel fondly remembers:

"Well, I actually learned a lot from Sam during our trip. I know many Holocaust survivors but he was different. First of all, he was the first Holocaust survivor I met who isn't from Israel. He didn't come here after the war. That was different for me, and I learned that you don't have to live in Israel to remember and perpetuate the Holocaust. I saw how much he loves and appreciates Israel, but yet he's doing an amazing job perpetuating the Holocaust memory in his country.

Another thing that I've learned about him and from him is his inner strength that he takes with him anywhere he goes. It was hard for him to go back there after such a long time, but he was so strong and he even strengthened us as needed. He was always there to hug, to tell, to share... He is such an amazing person.

Sam affected very positively my learning experience. By being there with us, waking with us there and sharing his own emotions, he made our thoughts and memories much more meaningful and emotional. He told us stories about the places we visited. What's a better way to learn something then being there and hearing a firsthand story? It was such an honor to be there with him. Having Sam with us was definitely an enriching experience.

Sam was AMAZING!!! He was our friend, our grandfather our teacher all at once. He laughed with us, he told us jokes, he hugged us whenever we needed and he has a very rich knowledge about many things. We all love him and very much appreciate him traveling with us and being there for us all the time. I sung a song in Hebrew in one of the extermination camps and after it Sam came to me and said: "I didn't understand a word, but I got everything. Thank you". It was one of the strongest moments that I had with Sam. He was an integral part of our group."

SOURCES

Bolivia, The Jewish Community." International Jewish Cemetery Project, International Association of Jewish Genealogical Societies, www.iaigsjewishcemeteryproject.org. Accessed 5 July 2016.

Golbert, Rebecca L. "Holocaust Sites in Ukraine: Pechora and the Politics of Memorialization." Holocaust & Genocide Studies Journal, vol. 18, issue 2, 2004, pp. 205-223.

Gradel, Morris. "Pinkas Hakehillot Polin: Krasnobrod." Encyclopedia of Jewish Communities in Poland, Yad Vashem, vol. 7, 3 Aug 2003, pp. 513-515. www.jewishgen.org/yizkor/pinkas_pland/pol7_00513.html. Accessed 25 July 2016.

Gradel, Morris. "Pinkas Hakehillot Polin: Tomaszow Lubelski." Encyclopedia of Jewish Communities in Poland, Yad Vashem, vol. 7, 26 Nov. 2006, pp. 237-241. www.jewishgen. org/yizkor/pinkas_pland/pol7_00513.html. Accessed 25 July 2016.

Pal-Mac People (1997, May). Pal-Mac Notebook: News From the Palmyra–Macedon School District, 16, (4), 13-14

Rind, Kresel. Holocaust Memoir. Translated by Debbie Rothman. June 2011.

"Samuel Rind: Seeking Refuge." The Meta and John Spiegler Holocaust Remembrance Lecture, April 28, 2014. Corning, NY. Amanda Killian, artist.

"Samuel Rind: Seeking Refuge." Social Studies Department of Steamboat Springs High School, Lecture, May 9, 2014. Steamboat Springs, CO.

Shapiro, Francine. "Pinkas Hakehillot Polin: Rava-Ruska." Encyclopedia of Jewish Communities in Poland, Yad Vashem, vol. 2, 17 July 2009, pp. 498-503. www/jewishgen.org/yizhar/pinkas_poland/pol7_00513.html. Accessed 26 July 2016.

Temple Beth El. Book of Remembrance, 2016-2017/5777. Rochester, NY, October 12, 2016.

Vinokurova, Faina A. "The Holocaust in Vinnitsa Oblast." Jewish Roots in Ukraine and Moldova. www.rtrfoundation.org/webart/UK-arch-d2.pdf. Accessed 26 July 2016.

"Zhmerinka." Encyclopaedia Judaica. Encyclopedia.com. www.encyclopedia.com. Accessed 17 April 2017.

"Zhmerinka." http://www.au.geotargit.com. Accessed 22 July 2016.